The Egyptian Codex

A Return to Modern Egypt
The Activation of our
Codes of Re-Union

Written by Seer
Andrea Elizabeth

Copyright 2020 Andrea Elizabeth
This book is copyright under the Berne Convention.
All rights reserved.
No Reproduction without permission.
Printed in the United States of America
ISBN: 978-1-7346885-4-2
CATALOGING INFORMATION:
Elizabeth, Andrea

_____

_____
_____

Filing categories:
OCC032000 BODY, MIND & SPIRIT/Angels & Spirit Guides
OCC011010 BODY, MIND & SPIRIT/Healing/Energy (Qigong, Reiki, Polarity)
OCC011020 BODY, MIND & SPIRIT/Healing/Prayer & Spiritual
BIO018000 BIOGRAPHY & AUTOBIOGRAPHY/Religious
SEL006000 SELF-HELP/Substance Abuse & Addictions/Alcohol
BIB020050 BIBLES/The Message/Study
Andrea's websites:
www.spiritualenergyhealingguide.com
www.beurownreligion.com
Facebook: www.facebook.com/andreaelizabeth2020
YouTube: www.youtube.com/channel/UCCX0V_sGJTh9wDZlA0WLPyA/featured?view_as=public
Patreon: www.patreon.com/AndreaElizabeth

Table of Contents

INTRODUCTION 1

1. THE HOLY CREATRIX: THE SACRED OM 3

2. THE ANKH OF LIFE 10

3. THE CAPACITOR OF THE LIGHT 13

4. REALIGNING THE INDIFFERENCE 17

5. TIMELINE CREATION/CREATRIX HEALING 25

6. THE ADMITTANCE OF SURVIVAL 29

7. SPIRITUAL SOCIAL CONDUIT 36

8. THE INITIATION OF QUEEN ISIS 48

Written from a place of deserted timelines for Grace to become fully bestowed back to us as forerunners or masters of time of solidarity as Creatrix.

Here we peek into our valiant Grace and demand the return of our testimony or heritage as common time placement by and through the codes of our forgotten Egypt to further along our character of the grand holiness. it is paramount to enforce our own rules about these as time fissures are created when one awakens to these codes and extra light turns on and you begin to grow into heaven.

Alas, we return, not to repeat our pharaos, but to learn through mischief and Grace upon which we once were held imprisoned upon. It is a difficult design to manifest when we are slaves to society. Then once our prison was sold, we formed an alliance with these codes to examine just how and why we were let down and led astray.

It has come forth that part of our heaven space was eliminated by and through the coaxing of demagnetization or reimagined parts of our soul. Seeming privy only to those of higher standards of Grace, when often times we forgot our holiness within.

Re-imagined Grace is our perfunctory power and we stand tall in this Grace to redesign our own holy manna and we shall re-image or re-design our life as such. With brilliant X's and O's and a trillion brilliant lights in form, we shall each endeavor upon our own platform of heaven to literally redesign our own duty of Grace. As Grace is our platform, she is also our super power.

We were once a powerful nation of Goddesses and now is the time to re-create our light and disallow the old powers of the mortal man. We shall now and forever more be known as Grace of Gods together as one bright light shining so brilliant that the Gods before us shall dim down unto our presence and we shall nevermore be ruled by disempower. We are Grace empowerment and generated only by our own desire of deliverance by more Grace and more power and more Grace and more power, ad infinitum.

We are the empowerment of Grace in time through our divine limitless encounters with the heavens. We each beseech this power within, so the cultivating of our presence is so very necessary to learn and to live. With each step we rise into a new virtue of the Goddess. Performing regally and sustainably within as this power has existed all along. Let it be so.

The Holy Creatrix, The Sacred OM

As we begin with a meaningful desire to sustain more power by and through our Grace, it takes exceptional Goddessness to be strong and dutiful. When in doubt, provide to yourself at your leisure the profound song or sound of Creatrix or of the Sacred OM. Here is a most satisfactory deliverance as one is at home with the OM.

OM-ing for power is distinctly more satisfying than hiding our gifts. We create even more power by this Sacred Om-ing of the holy Creatrix within. Human nature is one of life as heaven on earth so why not provide yourself with this Sacred Om healing to become a more powerful Goddess than ever before. The Sacred Om is a plentiful empowerment of your own holy soul vibrational method. There is no other like yourself, and as on a wide scale of tomorrows, there never will be. Become a frequent user of this form of Sacred Om-ing for the empowerment you wish to know and to feel. These sacred and powerful endeavors link to your very own homage and while practicing the Sacred OM it will sign to the universe that I am OM or I am home. This literally lights up our planet and circumvents light so that the power of amusement grows significantly inward. We lighten up and quit taking ourselves so seriously and become a forever Creatrix light. However many more lives one will ascertain, our Om-ing light will always prevail and you will return again and again to this Sacred OM-ing light and you will really begin owning your own Sacred OM.

Retaining this Sacred OM power is the only real pertinent part of Creatrix that holds our true sound or frequency. It is sometimes difficult as we as woman rein our power back to allow the so-called man of the house to take over or our lives or the motherhood to take front stage. We often forget that we are Sacred beings, and we forget our Sacred OM.

Coming home to our Sacred OM is like heavens abyss of light or Christ light, it is a calling to our soul space that has never even existed prior to now. This moment it is time to create your own Sacred OM.

Om-ing For Your Presence

Creating you own Sacred OM takes some practice, as no one really knows that it is inside of them. It takes time, effort, the clearing off your entire body, clearing your meridians, as well as your chakra system by and through the elimination of all aspects of the unholy. That means that the proverbial life you have known shall be redesigned into a healthy living space for all intents a purposes to be provided souly and holy to have as a liturgy of Creatrix.

Your own Sacred OM shall provide shallow resonance to those who have none and provide a living space for your own true essence to design a real and true living adventure for you. This perfunctory expression of your own wavelength will be a territory for living designed and creating a phenomenal existence for you and yours.

In Egypt we performed what we like to call a series of holy gestures to which we would call in all manners of home. Meaning that the heavens or what we were thought to be heavens were a desire for most of us to become our home or place of peace. Daily we would manifest days of harvest co-designing a deep solitude and resonance of Grace. We would bring in the holy heavens by designing our place mat with Grace as a sort of starvation system. If we did not have Grace, then we were starving. We were listless and predetermined to bequeath our Grace to the heavens each day, literally un-starving our self and being fed by this mammon.

Each day we would prepare a sullen plate of the Ankh of life to reinforce our light.

Grace upon Grace upon Grace was our culture and as woman we performed as such.

Grace was our literal superpower as when one was down, we would provisionary assist the others back up to our level of performance. It was Grace standing upon the backs of Grace as placeholders. So as such, we began to transform our living space as God through Creatrix in the morning performing the call up the heavens to bring peace upon this planetary earth. The more we performed with this ancient style, we created a placeholder of Grace for the morrows.

The Creation of Our Own Sacred OM

Provide an altar for Grace to uphold and to rise up with you each day. Your altar space should have a mat on which to provide safety and alignment. Next create a spiritual practice in which to adhere to on a daily basis and upon which Grace can be upheld fully and respectfully. Arc your dissonance with the Sacred OM and then perform your natural and daily occurrence of Grace upon which you live stand and breathe upon. Your own nature will provide you with the talent to use such gifts of performance.

Now a Sacred pillow is a great place to sit upon and allow this bond between you, heaven and earth. That way these each can reside inside while you are creating your next pertinent move up and into the power of enlightenment.

In your mind's eye begin to Create various circles or O's and put them into the mainstream by your own flow. Notice them in your daily meditation while you bring down the column of light simply add the O's to the white light stream of justice, as you are an empowered being of presence and each time you find yourself off a bit, show the world your own Creatrix as such.

X's and O's are objects in which to fathom creating. Sing this formulation of presence if you can. You can sort of perform your own magical synchronicities and formulate a new spectrum of creating. i.e., Abra Cadabra as I speak, it is so. Sort of like a formulation of time or a timepiece where you advantageously bring in an object to be seen, such as a lyolite or rainbow spectrum. You notice it, you connect or adhere to this frequency, and then you both enjoin in its frequency of light and then you take it into your frequency rhythm by abiding it a new presence in your soul space. The presence of a new frequency enhances your old space tremendously by opening and walking you home, once again to Grace. Each time you add a frequency to your light, you are creating and eliminating the shadowed existence that remained prior to you opening this book. Now you are an operative link to the heavens by performing your own sound as a prism regaining all that has been once forgotten.

Begin now by stating that: I am the presence of Grace through the holy Sacredness of OM going forth as part of a prism of sound light to love and Grace. This is my bounty, and I shall forevermore live here in this space for the Sacred OM is phenomenal and healing and I am its holy bounty of forever. I shine in this holy resonance and I bask in the beauty of Creatrix.

Thine bounty is in thine presence provided from Atlas' Godlike presence newly opening into his returning the present of the Sacred OM. Atlas was given the task of holding up the heavens as punishment from Zeus. Incidentally we are enjoining in his presence here today to solidify the terminal divined here we are open and forgiving yet insatiable and kind.

So, go forth with the next words of:
If thine eye be single, thine body shall be or live

in the fullness of light. Are all created as a sort of hand signal to the opening of time, however our bounty has been shimmery at best. It is now time to release all that had one held back our presence and allow for the timeline step into present time and work from that very dutifully and we shall regain our presence as God's Grace fulfilled in our timelines as duty to our own holy heavenly reside. This is our only holy presence that we need raise, it is a factor in time when our present timeline crimped and delineated to a new lifetime of unholiness, so now our presence is back once gain to be straightened out or filled in and this is our next part.

The Ankh of Life

Lineage Destruction in Present Tense

Diligence is key here to believing as we once determined that as a coward, we all had it something so to speak, but as a lion we take over the country. Notwithstanding our future sight we can reconfigure our past lineate and rediscover the newness in our light.

We can literally recompose our past lives as a sort of disenfranchised light of being and retraining our holiness. The Key here is to disenfranchise those old part of our existence and revive our Grace upon which we once lived and breathed from. It a case of stepping into our holy truth about us and tearing down the wall s we have built to increase our limitlessness by and through our Creatrix. We were all once Creatrix Goddesses, and the heavens still remember this. It is fortunate for us that we can disavow all that once was and reinvent ourselves as Creatrix Goddesses.

The simple prayer of Disenvowment Stepping into Perfection Timeline

I am forevermore disavowing all presence in which I had once omitted to dim my soul light in order to give someone else to folly. I now and forever disavow this from my presence and will never again allow it to comeback into a second sight of light for myself or any of my ancestors. It is heaven's gate that I now am provided for and step in to and by way of allowing in full Grace capacity I except my old arrangements in which I sold myself over in submission, I know remain in full control of my liturgy of Christ as a holy giver of life, as I am my own holy ankh of divine, and I begin to only ascertain that divisional aspect of me by and willfully agree to find somewhere in the past that I agreed to live less than I deserve, and now I step up and into my perfection timeline of Grace with all that is holy within. I shall never deny my capacity again as I am whole and in containment of my own divine Grace. I am all that is holy and discretely bring my past limitlessness up and into my holy capacity of a firm timeline of Grace whole and full and complete.

Feel the rise of this new vow of empowerment with the ankh of life rising up and through your first chakra all the way up and into your crown chakra and hold this space until you feel whole and complete. You will know it is complete when the flow comes all the way up from the 1st Chakra and flows easily up and through your body, then out of your 7th chakra, overflowing down your outer body. When you see yourself as a giant golden ankh, you will know the process is complete.

It is done, it is done, it is done.

Let it be so.

The Capacitor of The Light

Living in the Presence of our own Holy Creatrix Being
A Timeline of Preexistence Grace

With a full-on presence of God, we can now redefine our own holy presence in this timeline.

We can take advantage of how what when and where we found easy outs in our life to not have to hold this divine presence. Is only there where the mysteries lie. Where you sort of crept out of your timeline of healing, mismeasuring and revealing parts of us that were meant for something else.

Each time we stepped away from our path to take an easier road, we suffered immensely.

So now we shall have you honor your presence

at each of those times when you could have kept on the path but did not. Do your best to remember where you stepped off the line and create a list.

When you are complete, see the door in front of you.

Step in; what do you see you, what do you notice, who is around you. When I did this practice, the door that opened for me was metal shop class in school, I felt I want to build things but thought I would be ridiculed as a girl.

Now in this space open it up and see it in front of you as a path, then, sort of sew it together and perform a ritual and lose or drop it off to sort of step off and out of that particular path and create a new reconfigured straight path of Grace.

You can sort of erase it with your hand, then see it as a piece of paper, and crumble it into a little ball and return it to the universe, that way you path has been fixed unilaterally, not consequently.

Now behind that which you just energetically destroyed, is the path you should have taken. Now, just see this path in your minds eye and allow the energy to come in to your open space and refill you up as Creatrix. Feel this presence as your own nakedness.

State: I am filled, I am bathed and I am loved with this holy Creatrix presence. Repeat this until you are complete. It may take some time. Feel each and every energetic ping of each word, and feel it filling up your Creatrix lineage. Feel it over and over and allow it to fill up each part of you that you cleared out or that you forgot about. You will know when you are complete.

The bounty of doing this, is that you are provided with safety and a perception of home and the power of the light energy flows over you and protects you and enhances your light as you fill up with the bounty of perfection and individualized energy that was supposed to be yours in the first place, we are sort of going back and reclaiming our bounty of our light as we have given it away so many times.

Do this until you cannot see anymore doors. And continue to fill up your space over and over and over.

This reclaiming your bounty of light to create an encompassing timeline of −reclaiming your light of Grace and begin filing it up with such to be a cup runneth over with Grace living being.

See to it that all lifetimes or timeline are done with this if you can if not, do not worry keep it simple.

The forevermore prayer.

I recant any and all other prayers I may have

sought after when I was not filled with this divine Grace that is so rightfully and truly mine. I now adhere to this strict divine property of Grace within alignment with all that is mine in a way of perfection and now determine my fate upon this filled in and complete timeline of Grace. It is heaven on earth upon which I derive my passion from. All is over and forgiven and I am filled with the divine Grace of existence.

    Blessed be.

Realigning the Indifference

Combining Heaven through Hell, a Composite of Extramarital Division

Have you been married to something other than your soul? These levels consummate a bringing in of a say forestry of a divisional sight. Once you may have been married off to someone or were forced to do something and your soul literally vanished.

So, in this series we shall begin to validate what part of your soul needs refurbishing?

Note a time and place when you literally gave your soul over to a person place or thing in order to create a non-shame based decision, like you married someone because you had sex and you because you thought it was the right thing to do, or you began lying at a job to get ahead, or any and all situations where you were not fully in your truth. Lies create denying of our soul. This may take some time, don't rush. Begin listing any and all things that led you astray from your own persevering of your soul based existence. We all have this. Look at it in terms of years. 0-10, 10-20, 20-30, etc. Take a good look at your life in ten year increments, and really go over it from a higher level sight, and see those times where you lied, or felt shame or made decision because you "had to". Each time you went against your gut or intuition, your soul lessens a bit. This is why we do this practice, it is important to first, identify, then redemnify those lost parts of hope and return them to become whole.

So, when you have them all written down to view, see them all in a giant bubble, then begin to see the bottom flowing out of each of them and into the earth entraining a new "soul presence". Allow your old soul self or presence to indemnify, your Sacred truth. Feel it seeping in from your crown and washing away any and all old part of that old non-soul life existence, really feel it filling in parts that you literal gave away of yourself in order to get ahead, or not look bad or feel shame about some decision, really let it redemnifying all part of you that were not your own religion about you, your Creatrix alignment, your true soul purpose. Sit with this for some time.

And when complete, you know exactly the time and place you did all of this. Feel the layers of the different decisions you made concerning your soul light.

Imagine each particle begin redesign by the heavens to add the old consistency back and to return to the x's and ox's of creation. Your timeline awaits. Keep clearing your space until you feel complete.

Look for each time you lied, you stole, you created farses, to take the pressure off you and an all decision that created a lack of souls presence in your life.

This is a weary task, but so very necessary as you do this in your own presence you will recap each and every time you made the wrong decision for you soul's presence. This may take some time. You will know it is complete when you see a silvery mesh or manner come around your space, like silvery lava coming down into you presence.

When complete the ox's and o's will become the ankh upon which you reside in this existence

It will feel honorable, consensual and complete.

All memories the come up will be revealed in order to be healed.

Thake time on this one. I am free and a live amen.

Are we not an advantage taker? We think yes,

but quite the opposite we form new alliance within as soon as the old bastards are set free from our lineage.

Each divisional space replicates our honor as Creatrix. So, for this piece, we interpret our light as a sort of nonlinear exception and reformally rising to the occasion of how to form an alliance within our own deepening resonance to become one even more Creatrix like and more rebellious in terms of not letting our guard down any longer and beginning to return to our natural state of desire.

We can live in desire if we find it is all formed quite naturally and quite formally. We must divide the old into the new so as to sort of ascertain this was once me, but now I behold this, a presence as present. Get it?

Our lives are our present and a gift from our Creatrix so as to ascertan enlightenment for our own glory inside the glory of the presence of our holy Creatrix.

We are Creatrix Gods literally and formally and we can exhibit God-like features, but in order to provide a sound resonance, we must first be rid of all that once held us captive; because as captors we re-mind our divisionary minds that we are captive so therefore we cannot provide fruitfully or souly.

Our minds are a complete divionsary exception when it comes to our truth. As we all know, we have kept those old secrets, or shameful ideas about yourself or family, or what have you and they have not seen the light of day, until now. Today is the day, to release the captive memories you have brought forth once again, and from this day forward we will have a total, and complete open ended futility-less life, mind, body and soul and this is what has prevented us from our freedom. We have been in a prison in our own mind about absolutely every single thing we felt dishonored about. We have lived a dishonored life because of all the things that have dishonored or devalued your soul.

   A little lesson here about honoring:

   One time in Egypt there was a precise pharaoh whom had exquisite taste in men and jewelry; but his honor scepter brought or gave him harrowing excuses for not be allowed to be accessible to those young boys or men; and in turn, he decapitated all of the surrounding mentors who had made him feel undesirable, and less of a man for those absolute "real" thoughts. He beheaded thousands of men in order to keep him from the insatiable thoughts. Now the moral of the story here is self-acceptance not self-denial. Because, if he were to just allow for himself to be real, and true to himself, he would have saved hundreds of lives and thousands of heads. His own self absolving or self-hatred because of his own real desires kept in in misalignment with his ultimate truth of Tutankhamun.

He was his own ancestor and his beliefs were of the utmost accepted to the heavens of sorts, and if he lived any different, he would not fit in the ultimate life in which was promised to him, he would be a mere sultan. And his pride would not be allowed to live as such, he was a pharaoh, not a mere sultan. And many lives were lost because of this man and his story is of truth to so many as each bequeaths his own revelry for his souls and there are no changes what is true about one's self. If we deny even a smidgen of our own self-understanding we step across and away from our heaven space. As we behold a kingdom of the Gods within so as to become a manna of beauty. For the efforts of this piece let us understand that: Once we ascertain our Grace from which we flow, our bountiful reign begins, and until then, we shall not flourish as designed, we shall live a sultan life, and not the life of a pharaoh.

So, our greatest realization of our own worthiness or to be absolutely truthful to the point of harming our persona. If we live to be a certain aspect of what others think we should be, we are done. There life is over, and we can just come to the realization that we are in fact living a lie, and from this lie, we die souly in form on a daily basis. As we cannot perform at full capacity if we are lying to our self.

We must, and I say must again, must operate from the fullest of self-truths possible in order to divide our past from our future; we are hell bent on truth as a substance of all Creatrix God living.

Here in this 4th dissolution of self, we bring in the homily of self-care and the tactics for great forms of living our truths in Grace, even if it kills us, the old us- that is. A new life awaits as your own true heavenly manna is a sculpture of the morrows and you are to now prove the acceptance of your light as your truth.

Now as a provincial we shall sing homily to our old past assigned reign of design so as to cocreate or co mange or future soul self. As we disembark from our old self and step upon the boat onto the Nile and delineate all fissures of our past ideas of whom we were once supposed to be based upon the religion of our time, we now accept that we inside are all God in-form. And we all inside are all creation and we all inside are al perfection there is no other term for our presence other than perfection.

So, each lineage path that brought you here right now as you read this, is currently being dismantled as and into a perfection lineage back and back and back, and into the timeline of its creations. Think about it, one person after one person after one person, feelings, deceptions, lies, manipulations, etc., all are gone and being cleared out and a renewed into a perfectionary alignment with the heavens or God, or Creatrix. There is a timeline of perfection coming down the pike your way, so the old illusion of I am wrong, or I feel wrong, is over, and the new perfection lineage is created; you are the beginning of an endeavor most cannot endure, you are the product of consummation of the perfection of creations. We are all perfection inform. Not only heavenly, but systematically as one perfection growing off the other form of perfection, like the initial explaining of Pi; piece by piece, growing perfectly from the last piece of perfection, over and over and over and into infinity, this now you, eternally.

You are healed, you are heavenly and you are perfection; just being you will now almost become the outcast for some, but be strong in your alliance with your perfect space and keep moving forward as an isometrical perfectory lineage of light, coming from purity of divine creation. This is you. humanly perfection as discovered by the ancient Gods of the pharaohs. We are all one in divine line of perfection.

Blessed be.

Timeline creation/ Creatrix healing

The timeline of the pharaohs as time persists only in a mindset of the dissolutioned.

If we were to channel humanity then we would be growing at a distance unknown to man or society but once we step out and way from this linear thinking process, we can amply identify where we are at any given time, respectively.

If we see our life as a line, as we look down in the process of our Creatrix mind, we can see this line between our legs, running front and back in the axis of the morrows.

Looking down we can see where we or our families existed from the pharaohs backward and from this timeline we can begin to adjust our wares as such; if your family has a history of malnutrition, look back in your mind's eye, on the timeline and bring in justice to this particular part of your family lineage as a sort of magnified decision to fight for our food. Then simply sort of cover it up and move on. Look for each timeline where there was a struggle in your family history. Step into that timeline, move out the struggle, and fill it total and complete Grace. This will eliminate the struggle from there and clear it at all the way to the future of your timeline and your family's timeline. There is a now Creatrix God lineage more powerful than this timeline creation healing. This healing forms a bond within the bedevilment of our existence, each problem or bedevilments that show up somewhere in our family timeline, this work here sort of decompress the problems and angst and allows for an easier existence in time front or backwards.

Use this timeline adjustment to clear out heresies, deaths by plague, and any underlying previous existence diagnosis; this will be a use for our future race to clear backward then forward, thus not allowing in the old problems from our past existing lives.

Treat yourself well after doing this work, as you will be in total need of an adjustment in all aspects of your life. Just like in the movies, as we clear or move someone from the past, the present and future realign. So do your best not to do it all at once, you will be thrown into a loop of your existence and you will almost suffer certain circumstance, unbeknownst to you in present time. So slowly map out which kingdom you wish to be working with in present then rest for a time, so that adjustments can be made.

Using the exercise

X's and O's can be a game changer.

Step up and into a timeline, look for all the X's or all the O's. And do these at one time; then the next time look for the opposite one you used and work on that. This way all opportunities for the X's will be healed at one time and then the next time all the opportunities for the O's will be healed the next. Make sense? This allows for a straight line of healing.

What are the X's and O's exactly? They are timeline forfeiters. As each timeline has its own divinity Switch. Each time a person has distinguished a specific warranty of his life, it is replaced by either an X or an O. Not specifically however to entrain. Meaning that the X's are a superficial understanding where the O's are a more flatline or minute aspect of your soul. So the underlying veil of these two particular spaces, are really an under piece, or underbelly of the say beast. Each resonates its own variable also meaning that it does not matter who what when or why the individual sort of turned away from their Creatrix line, it more matters how the person acted therefore creating a different understated life. We use the X's and O's because this is an integer formed basically for the human sight to understand. It is a very simplicity language almost like binary. We hope this brings in a great understanding of the X's and the O's.

Blessed be.

THE ADMITTANCE OF SURVIVAL

Now forming this Alliance may not be so easy as it sounds as we have much old provisionary ideas of who we were always taught to be.

Understanding Ourselves as Spiritual Beings in form as Human

How this old ritual comes at a time when the form of this planet has Municipal boundaries almost as the X in Egypt where one could not practice their spiritual work without being tormented or killed or ridiculed. So we now offer this as a sort of timeline speeding up as or In-forming a new presence.

And in as much as your human self will want to keep going back to the old this new spiritual ramifications will be seemingly dyer that all the hope you once had may go out the window and you may have to start a new spiritual fight. During this process you will become magnified as sound to bring in a heartfelt magnification of creation and of all that is Holy.

Creation is felt throughout the universe almost as an Earthly determination of having to find the answers of x equals y. However, the creation frequency delves deeply within each of our DNA it resonates deeply with in all the planets and it forms a critical Union of the Stars. We are no longer silent we have great aptitude to bring and thank you Andrea Elizabeth for allowing us in.

Under this old recourse we have no creation space, however above the new one we have vigilance and a hearty idea of who we cannot become. No way can we share with you a great provide until we are certain that you are openly and Heavenly clear to what we are bringing forward. And in no way do we offer a clear concise aspect of humanness however, we do offer an open-hearted place of existence to identify the core beingness of Who You Are. Where can one live and have an aspiration to sing if one has no mouth? We offer a way out of the old human ways so that you may resonate within the human glory of God. Forever more as one within a true Creatrix space. For this next part we offer up a new intelligence that comes briefly from a futuristic timeline.

There are old harmful identifiers that try to bring in Old ideas and harm to your soul. In essence will you find it attentively necessary to divide Our Lives into three parts. Mind, body, and soul. Beauty, Joy, Grace, Love, Integrity, Humility. All three things identify aspects or parts of us which are heaven. And all things we articulated past knowledge as homeopathic beings coming forward. In a sense, it is a being or an aspect of God and light bringing homeopathic tendencies.

Starting with all that is Holy let us entertain any value upon our Creatrix. Let us understand now that there are no more formalities as we know now all things are trying to keep us separate as God. In essence we all form a very valuable instinctive space where we know deep inside that we are of great pleasure. We honor our own core as being a precise clear non-gated space of how we can become holy. In essence we app to begin a new valuable consecration of Creatrix.

Without this homeopathic agency we gain nothing as Source, we must understand how to become healed and most pleasurable to all things. As an Essence we must find what keeps this part of us limited. Undefined knowledge is misinformed interpretation. We find Surplus hidden deeply with

Inner Space and now we must find the void from which to live. From this void we find it superfluous.

One can only know God I am an outer knowledge. Now I understand the fight for which our forefathers fought. Undermining all values no longer we take this opportunity to form an alliance with our Creatrix within. Never before have we brought this forward as this timeline is an opportunity waiting to happen as there are so many awful upheavals happening now. There is no other way to State this. As you are now in a state of lockdown nobody can get out of their space without having to have feelings of who they are deep down inside. They are in this time we are in visiting the world as you know it as a place of a chalice waiting to be Sublime. Each Creatrix in lockdown shall in case a new trouble has so many no not know themselves Within so as a result many May flourish but also many may not. But the exception is always good and bad to every ideal now we bring into exception the value of what we have to offer a minimum of are days of Maximum silence for mind body and soul. There is no other way to define this. The value of all of this will be to incorporate your Holiness into your sight as well as creating a divisionary fastest within. The quieter we become the less we need to speak there for the more we are of value as presence living from this presence brings new opportunities and a valuable space of chaos. Moreover, there will be a situation in which one may need to reside in this quietness. For the record we have told you so.

In this next exercise let us bring into existence in our core of cores all that resides within our huge valuable Ascension lineage. We have tried this before and have failed so here goes. At this core value we must ascertain how to understand ourselves as God.

So, demean yourself no longer and bring forth the powerful initiation of Egyptian timelines. In this timeline we shall Endeavor a new lineage or Link to the Past.

See yourself in the middle of the pyramid allowing all of the frequency to entrain your entire body space act as if it is a crystal bowl going around and around and this frequency and vibration is entraining you to your very core and as a symptom you may allow your body to simply just fall off or step out of it and then unzip yourself and allow this old body to just go into Mother Earth. As you are listening to this sound of frequency going around and around like a crystal bowl you give yourself the permission to bring back absolutely every part of you as your ascended higher self from Egypt until now and allow in every part of magic, and your gifts to be retrieved and brought into current time so that they will allow you to have a fantastic wonderful life now. There needs no further explanation on this. This is a continual exercise to practice and to inform your ascended higher self that your are present now in present time, currently 2020 and all gifts be bequeathed to you at this time. There is no turning back we are freeing the alliance within. Blessed Be.

Egyptian Code Exercise

As part of our code we now identify our precise code or frequency lineage to our soul. Imagine yourself in a giant Egyptian pyramid having it swirl around your head all the way around until it goes down into the earth and its planted as it is planted into the Earth feel it swirling around you and allow in your old Visionary space of who you pretended to be, to be dissolved and allowing this magical Essence to be brought down into every fiber of your being. Each cell is being upgraded. Each and every light cell being terminated and upgraded as your DNA consists of new strands and lining up your new Egyptian codes. From this day forward you will never rely upon the old parts of you again. Continue to allow these new Egyptian codes to upgrade you and become one in alliance with all that is. You never have to step back again.

You cannot. Ground yourself into the Earth and into this pyramid and then allow the pyramid with yourself to go into the Earth expand and disintegrate. You are now one with all that is Holy. Blessed Be.

New Egyptian Code Prayer

Heavenly Divine, I now reside in your presence as Holy Creatrix from this day forward. I have at last become an open channel for all that is Holy within. My Divine Essence is grounded and materialized within our Earth Mother and now has become part of me as human.

Every single X and O resides deeply within my space and I now am a coinciding part of the universal mind and guiding myself into the heavens above. Have Thine Eyes been opened?

Spiritual Social Conduit

As part of Creatrix we have been asked to become a spiritual social conduit. How have you brought this forth in your life? Are there values in which you have not met yet? Is there a way in which to change the course of your past? Here we bring forth into present time a way into your past where you once held a position of grandeur. We Now open up the space and timeline of Egyptian codes for you to step in deeply and to realize that you too are God within. Allow yourself to be honored in the spiritual manner as you can see deeply within the essence of all that is. Each Egyptian code shall become a force into your space and you will eventually resonate at Top Value. Begin seeing the X's and the O's in your daily life and understand these at each time you see when you shall be upgraded. Your eyes are becoming aligned with the precise perspective of the Egyptian Codex. From a higher sight, we gain a higher understanding as well as a higher view of our presence. It is at times difficult for some to be bequeathed this sight as they have huge guilt for their parity. Timeline understanding is a way of harmonizing our culture. If you have ever had that feeling or thought that, I am a queen, why does no one see me as such? You have this because in one or many of your lifetimes you held a reign. It is now time to bring such reign back and to live in our sovereignty. That is what the Egyptian Codex is designed to interpret. That piece of you and or your lineage that has been lost in time. Bring that forward into current time and let your Creatrix design a new life for you and your family.

Once you have seen the X and the O at the same time you will know you are finished and complete. This will have a different meaning to each of you reading this book because no one sees the same. You will simply know or be told intuitively. Then the next value will come and the highest and shiniest of blessings will be brought to you. The more you value yourself and live deeply within your essence of Creatrix, the more light will be shining upon you. There will be no more running, you are found. Our Egyptian codes have been codified to begin to bring in and make sense for our lifetime. In this endeavor, we can now open our heart mind and soul to the missing piece of our soul in this lifetime. The X and O together create the Living Ankh and that is why they will be brought together, for you to see the obstacles removed. Looking at the symbol, it almost makes sense. This living ankh has been brought into our awareness to raise our divine presence and our divine frequency. Our lineage has been kept down up until now. As we now rejoin each and every lineage of Sisterhood, we form a new Bond and bequeath to ourselves the heavens deeply Within. Now is the time to enjoin within and with each other as a Sisterhood and become a high priestess of forever. Join in our Sisterhood of the masses in order for the new line or lineage of Creatrix to be reborn and become sufficient as a power in our lifetime. There shall be no more ruinous platforms from the old as this new light has encompassed all in all of our presiding deaths. Our physical death by day returns our spiritual lineage. Now returning to the death of our old self by which we now entrain a new source of life for living.

    The ideas of the X and O's has now begun to make sense to me and I now share them with you. Creatrix's carry the XX chromosome and in time it has been a sort of "greatest mistake" to overpower them. Them meaning the XX chromosome. Individualization of the female anatomy for singular uses has driven down the need for more power amongst the women of time. In order to alleviate and have the women of power succumb to the rape and even murder of our scorned leaders, the irrationality still continues to this day as men have literally taken over the laws of the land and infiltrated our brethren. In a singular decade the men have demolished a power trait in women by never ever allowing them to flourish as they once did in Egypt. In Egyptian time, men and woman new of the power of the Goddess. And exuberated their goodness. Never was an unspoken word whispered as to how the men could overtake the powerful women and Goddess. It was a literal given to be one with the earth mother and to provide for an aftershock if any man did rise his head to strike. It had once been a legion of premarital or primordial existence as Goddess power was so fully empowered. Never once to be looked back at as some how to be taken, so the telemerose of our genetic at one point has been dishelved or almost put away of sorts and that new power or piece has not been allowed to rise until now. We are the power. We now rise. We now step back from the dead and rise to our power, the most full occasion of our rights as our telemerose of or genetics has stated or brought forth those to speak.

    Our **XX** helix admits to our sources as power in literal numbers and the duplication of such particles of power has now been reawakened and we now rise to our own insurmountable objectives to become once more empower or in power. We are no longer, encamera so to speak we are up front close personal and ready. What we offer here today now is power in full frontal ability as source enthralled upon our Creatrix. She is ready to show up, be counted. Activate and strongly decide how to reawaken or re-live our times as Creatrix, Goddess or simply power.

All powerful beings are now present once again and we state the prayer of allowance to be unified within our own troubled past and our existence is now more crucial than ever as the man made world is starting to crumble from within as the power the men think they posses is shallow and it goes not beyond their capability of being able to handle the offensive of our taking back our literal power of existence and standing tall in our own superior resonance as XX helix beings. We offer up today a change or way into your goodness. We bring in a community of phenomenal power against the literal raging machine. As I sit and write this I just had the realization that this month, I am twenty years sober and you guessed it, XX. Wow. I have been putting this book on hold and now I know why. The creator has a great sense of humor. And now I rise! We are reawakening those sacred forces that have been hidden for centuries. The forces within our bodies was not lost in time. They are present as the present can be and we are strong together as One-Force. We now bring forth and reawaken our senses as Creatrix Force and the illusion of the man is lost and broken. We as world leaders now sanctify our presence as a world Creatrix Force. We now offer up a way in.

The Way in Prayer

As a prayer now, get into your still space within and watch your breathing. Watch it come in and watch it go out just like the waves of the ocean. Effortlessly breathe in and effortlessly breathe out. Do this for approximately 5 minutes in order to still your mind.

As you are doing this breath practice, imagine a golden Goddess force washing over the outside of your being and sort of just running down the sides of your body like a honey substance. Let it feed into your sour for the five minutes you are meditating.

Feel it seeping into your pores and feel the sweetness of this Creatrix Reign returning to you that is centuries old. Feel it seeping into your pores and allowing the sugar like substance to sweeten the cavities of your soul. Let is seep deeply into your upper heart soul reside and open the insides of your Creatrix to be once again revived with life. Sit here and breath with this for a bit.

Next as you are allowing this to take place, in your mind's eye see the Goddess sitting in front of you and allow for her to feed you the Golden Ankh of Life. Watch it come into your mouth and into your presence within and allow for it to return to its home and allow your body and image to become the Eternal and Living Ankh. Like it never left. Feel it coming back home to the mother. Let it come in and reset your old being and allow this bread of life to feed your soul resonance and to reinstate your past homage or ideas as Creatrix. We are now uplifting your Telemerase XX Helix Integrity to now insist upon these two forms of existence. Sit with this for a while.

The more you form this crucial bond with the light, the more the double helix XX will procreate and reunify your soul resonance as when in the time s in Egypt we as woman were taught to rise by taking in the formidable ankh of life and creating an eternal existence to now rise. Well today is this that day ladies, today we rise.

Sit with this for a bit. What is happening is that we are forming an absence of pharos, we no longer have to follow their rulings we create our own by simply becoming more alive. As you do this practice more and more, you will find that the obstacles will disappear out of your life and you will hone in on your talents and you will be restored to your original state of existence, perfection. That is the image of these writings. That is the reason I have been told to write. To reignite the passion of the continuum in time. To go forward and reinstall this timeline piece that has been literally stricken from our history and the woman were never allowed to be written about. Our power cannot be harnessed as they once thought. We are the life givers, we are the breeders we literally do not need men in power. We hold the existence to the future in our existence and in our Telemerse values state as such. Yes we need men for procreation, but nevertheless we are undervalued no longer. We will teach our young to use their power, we will remind our adolescence they have healing capabilities, and we will remind the ones who are asleep that it is time to awaken and to rise up and become in power. Our time has come to reinstall our sense of value as one living organism of the truth or true existence in pure form not readjusted or fake form.

    An explanation of how this re-establishing of frequency works is that when a person or thing dies their energy does not die it just changes form into ether and the goes out into the universe somewhere-some how and during the time of that period as like attracts like, all energy from that specific timeline conglomerates together as form and apparently waits for the right time to come back and assist those from that period who have reincarnated and are ready to re-inform their same souls self and ignition is born. I am also being shown that this may have tried to happen at one time in history or another but there was not enough awoke women as they were all kept "under wraps" so to speak. But alas, now is time to rise and be INFORM and state this following intimate and antecedent or primordial awakening prayer or liturgy:

I (state your name) now in-form myself as Creatrix and now ask for assistance from my higher ascended being/self to re-entrain the value of my soul self existence into now and to bring in those parts of me that are fragmented in the universe as matter, particle matter and source. As I now call back each and every time period energy and cadence that will allow me to rise above the captive old frequency as martyrs for anyone. Any time period or anything. I am all aspects of my Creatrix Soul Self now and I call back all thoughts, emotions, feelings, words, denials from any parallel lives I am currently coinciding with and bring it all forth and into this now version of my soul. Imaging your body as a magnet, and then take a deep breath and breath back all those parts of you into now and hold them into your upper heart or soul reside. Stay here for a bit and really breath them into your body and soul. Next as you are in this process, see the XX helix being upgraded and carried forward from time into now to permeate any and old incarnated ides of when you felt you could not rise up. Feel this duo coming right into your person and swirling around and cleaning you off energetically and allowing all old parts of you that have not quite risen yet. Let them make their way in and around and through your entire being. This process may take a while, just be with it.

These giant XX's may need to shrink or separate or change form in order for your body to recognize these pieces of the work. So just be gentle with yourself and let it allow it in and to work with you however the energy needs to. Everyone is different so just let it happen. You will know when you are complete. You may feel it going down your spine to upgrade your double helix there, or into your 3rd chakras to replace your sense of powerlessness, and definitely into your 2nd chakra and power up your uterus as this is the power of God in action. Our inform and incarnate as women bring forth the power of creation in our being. That has been tossed away and locked up for so many centuries, that this is really what the entire book is about, restoring our fate as creators. Holding space as God in the interim for our usage of our own human existence as Creator Gods or Creatrix. This is and has always been our plight here. We were once owned, and yet now we are set free. This is our spiritual sexual and liberation of our sacred union as One Creator God Soul. Here we can mange to uprise together and to enjoin in our own willfulness which is not fantasy it is world resonance. That is key here. To cleanse our soul at a level as done never before. As I am writing his I see a XXX set helix where we may not need men any longer to procreate that is what the binary adjectives/objectives (not sure) are coming in and out. They are the key. We are key world leaders on a perfunctory existence into our primordial creation. We have found the key to our entitlement. It is almost as though we have been on a game of finding our truths and now we have found our most logical term for our life. Creatrix of power. I bring this today to enjoin in our fight for female justice and empowerment. I bring this in today for human decency to all women, not just the 1st class countries, all women - and here is why this is so very important, the more each one of us rises, we bring back ALL of our power from ALL of our lifetimes as we are creators of reciprocity and we can allow the other women the same rights just by rising and doing this for them as well as our selves. It is true, the more we are on the same cadence, the easier this will become. We shall rise as one free nation as the Creatrix in form. We finally have a stay or placeholder on this planet. The old planetary conjunction of male leaders male officers, male everything will now even benefit from our sight, as it may take the pride and justice of their holders for one. They have had to uphold this frequency for far too long. They have been developed also. So, when we rise as one, we rise together and in doing so, we rescind all old parts of our past existence and now radiate as the Radiant Goddess Isis.

   Blessed be.

The Initiation of Queen Isis

The taking of the temple within by storm. Today we bring in an idea of cataclysmic adventure an idea of the storm; YOU. You are the storm. You are a hidden light so deep and forlorn that you can't even see it with your human sight. A new dawn is present and today we call upon it to be given to you and upon the shoulders of our sisters. It is an offering of the Christ or holiness or God or Goddess aka Creatrix.

Obtaining Your Relic of Times Past

Our offering to you this day is to find out what part of the key you left behind in other lifetimes. We offer for you to embellish your own work or ways as such.

Beginning with a slight mediation of God within

and embellish it with a sight to become increased so as to feel the presence of ISIS within.

Open a space where you once held the golden form. In your mind's eye, see yourself as a key or as the Goddess ISIS.

Slowly and simply bring your vision to the top of your head and identify your soul space as a Goddess place of rest. Simply just ask to see it or for it to be seen. Now see ISIS there, right on top of your crown chakra.

Breathe new life into her and accept her presence as you now.

Sit with this for a bit.

Next, expanding your breathe as you breathe in, begin inhaling in and out that golden forever part of you. Creating a flow of forever. Continue to flow this golden forever breathe until you feel a wholeness or a golden embodiment.

Now, after you have become whole, ASK Isis to assist you to let go of All pieces of your humanness that do not correspond with this frequency. Bring in her healing aspects and continue this process until you feel wholeness or a golden embodiment.

Continue this defragmentation of your human body until you are completely golden.

Breathe everything off your human body until you feel free. This breath exercise may take some time, don't rush it. Use your imagination and your intuition. Isis will guide you as well.

If you want a different approach, see yourself as an ice cube melting into mother earth until you become a Golden Goddess in-form.

You will know this is complete when you feel a honey like substance run over you all the way to the feet and you will feel whole.

The Temple of Solomon Relic Return

Part I

Next, As the embodiment of Isis, I want you to go to the temple of Solomon and ask for your relic back from the ages. Ask to be shown Solomon's Temple, see yourself on the steps of the Temple, then step in and ask. This Relic will be in form of what you feel is yours, or your own Relic. You will know it by how it shows up to you and how it feels to you.

When you receive this age-old Relic, bring it into your heart space and put it back where it belongs, into a space that you were trying to fill with all the other things than you.

As you put the relic back into that inner heart space, see all wounds that correspond to this space and clear it line by line, piece by piece relationship after relationship.

Fit it into the perfect hole that was once left behind up to now.

Sit with this and feel what is happening, see what ideas, feelings, demonstrative being comes to mind.

Take notes if you need to. Sit with this for a bit, 5 minutes is good but 15 minutes are better.

Part II

Then as you breathe this relic back into your existence allow it to freely bring you answers to you own lifelong questions.

Why -____

Why____ and really become identifiable in this work. The more questions, the deeper your healing.

Part III

When questions are complete, go back into the Temple of Solomon and ask to be revealed to you what your part of this journey is here. Ask to be shown what part of you is left in this lifetime.

These will be Distinguishable only to you.

If you do not get an answer or vision go into the temple and simply allow for your essence to become part of the temple and easily make your way back and into the space for a while and have a conversation. Whatever comes to you and is relatable to your human self now.

This may take more time, sit and ask question, write them down.

We are in a full-on experience of latentness (existing but not yet developed or manifest; hidden or concealed).

In this exercise, we are bringing back parts of us lost for centuries.

Each time you do this you upgrade your Creatrix space.

– A Spiritual Practice -5 minutes within the Temple of Solomon

Play around with this exercise by turning yourself into air or ether, allow your body to turn into cloud form and to expand and to seek new levels of enlightenment.

This where you will often be sent to for more education as spirit.

This new work shall call each of you differently, for different reasons.

And the more you do this the easier it will become. And the more answers will be revealed.

Breathe in all the new knowledge and simply let it fill your space.

When complete, Step out from the Temple a full knowledge wellbeing.

Temple of Isis Reveal

Find the Temple of ISIS and upon the steps of the temple ask that your new soul be revealed to you. See yourself as a whole embodiment of Grace with this Relic in your heart space.

Then move into the temple and find the room in which you stay.

This shall be your new sanctuary, this is where you realign on a daily basis to find new relics of the past and pieces that have been hidden from you for centuries.

This is our new golden age of enlightenment.

Calling Back Prayer

I am now asking that each part of my spectrum be called back and into the timeline of Isis as One Goddess present now in current time.

I now call back all aspects of me appertain directly to the Goddess Isis and we now form a singular bond with each other.

We can now categorically be One or as One Goddess Isis in-form and become relations in-form to bring our Grace upon many Others. Here we form a bond of sight, sound and monikers. Having one single sight - I as Goddess Isis In-form.

I now light the flame of the Goddess Isis flame and turn the flow of the flame up to high.

Some may feel the warmth of the flame, see the fire bits or burning piece of this lifetime float way like burnt paper.

As I light this flame in your first chakra, image the purple flame coming up your entire body core and burning away all old pieces of you. If you want to turn up this flame, reach your hand out in front of you and grab the round knob and turn it up to the right, to turn it down, turn it to the left. Keep this flame hot and fiery to enhance you new journey.

Sit with this for a bit.

Let it be your desire to have more of this is a flame within so as to have this alive without

You and Isis as twin flames so to speak

Offer each other a new paradigm light

And the more we each work in this light,

The brighter each of us become within this temple of ISIS.

So now you need to manage your identity as Isis as a Goddess in-form. We do this by:

- Treating yourself well
- Talking to yourself as Goddess Isis
- Honoring your Goddess Isis space in this work
- Creating a bounty of light wherever you go
- Clean eating

- Clean house living space
- Clean water
- Green vegetables
- More ideas of Grace in your mind, less problems,
- Drama, News, Tv

Set out on a new journey of hope for your light to shine brighter and brighter and to become a beacon for those who have been lost with no hope. You may be the only light the lost ever see.

So, the more you act upon this work becoming Goddess Isis in-form, the more changes will be present in your life and in your loved ones' lives. The more you shall find inner love and peace and enchantment.

Until we meet again,
Blessings.

Stay Hopeful and Begin Opening the Door to the Past

Daily meditation shall consist of:
Stepping upon the halls of Isis going into your home and seeking a new piece of you each day.

These are simply parts of your power you let or

gave a way in this lifetime and other lifetimes.

Then go to King Solomon's Temple, find your body as air or essence then express that you wish this part of you to be revealed so that your human desire can be actuated within and so that you can see your new path of the day.

All will be revealed to those who come to remember. We all belong to each other as One.

So, if you cannot do this for yourself right now, do it for the others as One.

Do it for us as One Golden Goddess Isis

As we create a new Bond within our own Heaven space, we allow each of the particles of our own Nation so to speak to regain and be reborn once again as the almighty Isis Goddess as One. Our Heaven Space is Reborn and Alas We rise!

Our antiquity being is a profound lineage of divine light beloveds. There are no two ways about this, we are light regardless of what we have been told. We are allowing the light so deep inside of us to be reborn. The nature of our being is to become this powerful presence in current day.

Prayer

Prayer for this last part is, as I now bring heaven into my Holy Ankh space, return to my heart peace, joy and love and allow it to resonate to my core. As

I now undo each and every particle that has ever been entrained into my space to disavow my lineage. I now operate from a New Freedom deeply within my core and I now ignite my own Isis Flame deeply within my first chakra. As I bend down and I light this Eternal Flame, I turn the knob to the right and imagine this beautiful purple flame just burning up through my core and really burning off the old programs of the old lineage and to undo any and all parts that have been kept down and unused or and vowed as me. As I turned the knob to the right, I continue to burn up any and all old programming ideas, thoughts, frames of mind that kept me stuck on hold or in an addiction or whatever that looks like.

    I now as Goddess Isis stand tall within this burning of the purple flame within and begin to allow in each and every X and O from my lifetimes in Egypt to entrain my being and to upgrade my DNA to become this One Holy Goddess of Isis.

    Now this vow is never to be taken lightly. It is a very distinct piece of humanity. Each particle that once was Goddess Isis in each of us had been turned off, burned out, put out, turned off and disvowed. Now we recreate our timeline as Goddess Isis deeply within our core as One God for all eternity. We Now operate from a Divine frequency ridding ourselves of all delusions of being less than the frequency of Creatrix or God or divine. Stepping into our life as Goddess Isis and allowing this purple flame to flow and continually wash out anything that does not serve us as a sovereign being. This allows us to go forth and allow our sovereignty to bring in new light as others may need the same Awakening. One light to another to another to another. And all sovereignty as one Divine being the Goddess Isis.

There is nothing so far that has offered this to us and as many may come and many may not it does not matter, what does matter is that this frequency be held and live and breathe through us with the link of Egypt as our own inner God or Goddess Isis whichever you may wish to call it, but as we are upgraded into this frequency really imagine your life as Goddess Isis stepping into your suit as Isis every day, then seeing the world through her eyes and becoming one piece with all that is reimagined. As you live your life this way every day you will become comfortable with living this frequency of Goddess Isis. After you have become super comfortable doing this we ask that you turn around and see yourself Through The Eyes of Isis to begin to understand your core of where you live and where are your Sacred Ankh resides. The more that you see and connect to this link heart to heart from your outer self to your inner self and Live from that holy space, there is nothing you cannot accomplish. There is nothing you cannot do. There is nothing you cannot be. Be one with all that is comfortable ask and be one with the Goddess Isis.

We shall forevermore be grateful for those who come to this exercise. There is more to fathom and our next piece so become fully aware of your Goddess Isis Divine sovereignty self and live as such until we meet again.

Blessings.

www.ingramcontent.com/pod-product-compliance
Lightning Source LLC
Chambersburg PA
CBHW071254070526
44583CB00017B/2468